Poetry

Via Marisol

Poetry by Paul J. Bean

Photography © 2023 Paul J. Bean

Back cover photo © 2023 Blossom Blue Photography
www.BlossomBlueStudios.com

Book Design by AGP Digital Marketing, LLC
www.StudioAGP.com

For more information visit www.PaulJBean.com

Manufactured in the United States of America
ISBN-13: 979-8-9882734-0-0

Publisher: Touch Not a Catt LLC
Long Beach, California

Books by Paul J. Bean
Confessions of a Latter-Day Cynic

Screenplays
Thirteen
Night Must Fall

Plays
Another Time, Another Place
As I Am

Foreward

This book began as a document of my life here in Los Angeles, hence the name, *Via Marisol*—it's as much a geographical reference as an emotional one. I began the work many years ago, but sadly put it aside, until just the right combination of people (and circumstances) arrived in my life to inspire this project's revival and give it the shape and direction it needed.

Via Marisol is a monument to the many women in my life—the commendable, the commanding, the confounding.

I'm sure I'll meet many others who will help define the next several chapters of my life, but for now, my thanks, appreciation and love to the women who've been part of the journey so far.

Paul

Contents

Photographs

Content Warning

This book contains profanity, and well as references to generational trauma, domestic violence, and child abuse.

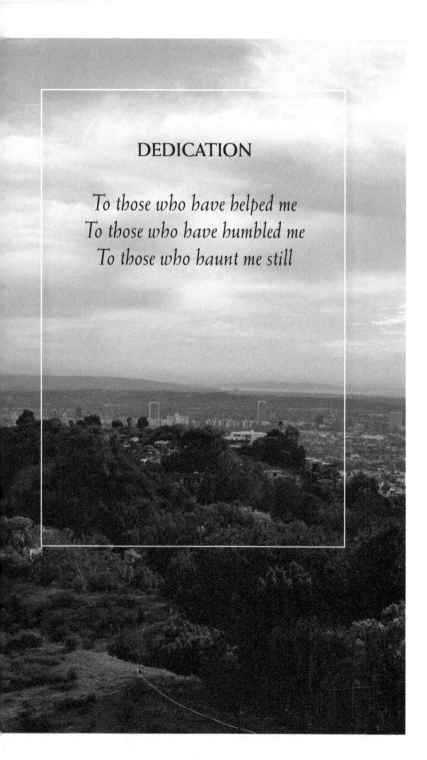

DEDICATION

To those who have helped me
To those who have humbled me
To those who haunt me still

Montserrat

Dearest daughter, tell your mother I love her so
The miracle you are makes her belly glow

A hue so strong it's life-force becomes a song
Chanted rhymes roll off her clever tongue

A puzzle to unravel, a wonder to hear
Primordial passion produces a tear

As my hands come to rest on her belly,
Tidal emotions wash over me so steadily

I feel a chill and my hands tremble slightly
The cosmos within, solemn and mighty

So captivated am I by your arrival, your future,
I almost forget to engage your mother's humor

Then again, the knowing glint in her laughing eyes
Keeps me speechless for a good long while

Hands

Flour-covered, kneading in dough
Washed under gushing water
Scraping skin through countless dish towels
Caressing with creams until the life comes back

Holding hands, perspiring on a hot day
Gripping jars and flexing muscles
Wringing them tautly to match furrowed brows
Tapping musically in time

Cradling a head, heart or pair of hands
Offering a pulse to those that need it
Giving a handshake to those who don't
Scolding a child or chiding an adult

So many years of service in a pair of hands
Hopefully freely given, never inured
Whether scaly or smooth, silky or scarred
Does their appearance betray their years?

Nike apteros

you lead, breasts forward,
arms arching out and back
flying boldy into the ether

neither smiles nor charm
delay you, so far so clever
against what and whom to heed

headstrong, miles ahead
of the boys in the button-downs
and the drabs in dungarees

would we see a smile
grace your face
if we could catch up to it

or are you so far beyond
sprinting winged foot over foot
youth usurping wisdom

you climb into a celestial ceiling
and like one with the night
stars shine through your eyes

celestial breeze becomes your breath
robed in galaxies of night
you take your place in the heavens

The empty bed

How can four corners of fake goose down and foamy gel
Cradle a partnership that descended into hell?

Back to back and should to shoulder
We should have turned and said it was over

Instead we stayed silent, pensive and still
As if layers of blankets would thaw the chill

Blood droplets on cotton christened a marriage
A trickle turned into a stream and then the miscarriage

Clawing through four hundred fifty thread count
I went looking for love and instead found doubt

But it was a strange comfort to find at last
After so much time lost I don't regret what's passed

Our bridal bed sadly fell apart on the loom
Yet birthed a brutal honesty, saving us from a tomb

Frailty

Frailty, so odious in plain sight
To everyone but the frail
A marriage of fear and need
A mockery of what should be held dear

Thy crime is overly simple
But I know you'll never ask
It's too much work to keep
The schadenfreude up

Name a penance and I'd love to give you one
But I already know you're silently paying it
Which returns round to hurt me
And damn it, that makes me mad too

Is there a way forward amidst all this pain?
I know there's an answer, I just want you to say
You'll reconsider, you'll strive, you'll discern
All the things you've instilled in me to learn

Woman thou art loosed as the good book says
I know that's about forgiveness (or perhaps a better way)
To deal with your foolishness, I need to mention
Please come to your senses, I beg and pray

.: Southern California :.

Mission Unknown

Stirring the embers

I'd almost forgotten your smolder
A slow burn, flickers of mischief and grace
Dance lightly across your pretty face

Popping embers fill the smoky air
Snowlike, it floats wildly before it falls
Covering man, woman, beast—sinners all

Glowing notes signal the heat below
No need to search for flames—they never died
Just buried beneath years of soot and lies

The fire was lit amid pockets of stolen time
And e'en far off fields can't dull the embers glow
Do you wonder which one of us misses the other so?

Time fumes forth a gauzy smoke surrounding us
When you're ready again to fan the lingering flame
Do you wonder—will we ever be the same?

Un femme mariée

if i could slow her movements down
between long drags of the cigarette
i think maybe, perhaps, i'll see a glimpse
of the wound within, not the scar without

smoke cadences spiral around long locks
carving question marks in the air

languidly i watch, hundreds of frames per second,
my attention fixed on her cigarette's two-fingered perch

burdened with her own world's worries
she stares deep into her cocktail glass,
chunks of ice watering down her drink
cheap cherries sweetening an already sour mix

Woke

Oh child, yer woke is broke
As fucked as your moral compass
Smash against a hard head
It produces a blisteringly blank slate

Not that you care—when you met him—
The man who would help you sell your soul—
He tried to kiss your eyes open, but
You live in a mirrorless house

The world through your eyes is judgement
Where it should be grace
When you look back at those you've left,
Do you know through which face?

Mamí

mamí, i talked to a boy today
no, he wasn't my husband ok
he gave me a gift so unusual
he told me i was beautiful
not in my face or the rest of me
but what he thinks is a bit feisty
he told me in my eyes he sees
sadness, maybe a life not free
but when i speak, my voice is a fight
a proud alarm, a search for what's right

mamí, i told him i don't feel sad
but when the words came out
they didn't have the truth he had
i thought about it for days and weeks
trying to clear my mind of fears and doubts
i think i know what it is i seek

it's the freedom of being not in love
with others but just with me
i don't want to constantly put above
people who don't deserve it you see?

mamí i know its hard with your generation
it was different then but you too can be free
i hope our *esposos* understand our situation
but even if they don't, i now know we can choose to be

.: **Santa Ana, CA** :.

Dia de los Muertos

Humane resources

Across an oblong desk
You sit, smirking
Lipstick pink and glistening
Nervous glands at work
Swallowing, lumpy throat
Betrays a calm front

Tap tap tap, your nails
On glossy wood, the laquer
Revealed in chips and prints
Of your agitation

Clearing throat, the thrush
Of your cheek glows,
Your orafice opens and
Thus spake the diplomat:
"We've had some complaints about you…"

Wicked

I

Blood marks the spot where the wall greeted my head
Trickling, tea-like...does the wall feel pain as well?
Let me sit—lie down—my collar is ruined...
I have to clean it before he...

II

My first sons' eye-daggers hurt more than my red cheeks
I assure him I can see through swollen eyes
I try to choke back the tears, but...God...
He says he doesn't believe in Him anymore, I'll pray for him

III

My second sons' second sight sees all, and he seethes
The burden of not being born the first, I suppose
So many eye-daggers to soothe, and so young
How long can I put off the part with the birds and bees?

IV

What was our third sons name—i mean teacher's name?
We got the call, it's not the first, ri...? Mmmm yes of course
Corn fields in the distance, you can see from the window
Stretching out, fanning—he did what?

V

Was it Cain who was Able to kill or maim to Cable?
Ha! Our fourth is now being cut out on a table
That rhymes in the worst way—what is this drug?
It ties my tongue, no tubes, well, I wish you were hung

VI

Our fifth, well, I guess I hardly remember that night
A grasping, clenched Hallelujah, the chorus sobbed over me
A slurred *apologia pro vita sua*, i know you like it rough
But your bellicose symphony can be heard in all hallways

VII

I promised [redacted] i wouldn't cry after it was finalized
The kids seem happy, my bed seems...empty
Like countless promises made, ones never kept
Like that bitch with whom you say you've never slept

VIII

You're not my Messiah, but my how the chorus swells
You look so good in your suit and tie my love
Tall, rugged, slicked back hair, so commanding
I am amazed by...wait...not in front of the kids...

IX

I promised [redacted] i would dry the kids' tears
After we got back together again
All the promises he's promised he will fulfill
Why does two look at five with such ill?

X

Yes my love we'll show them all, this time so different
Hope springs eternal when such a love we have is ours
You take my hand, darling, wait, that's my wrist...who's crying?
Shush dear, those are tears, not blood, I should know

.: Downey, CA :.

Korporate Amerika

Golden girl

The oldest saying ever told
All that glitters is not gold

A slit of sunshine parts your lips
As your smile starts suddenly
And cracking to crowning
Is but a millisecond

The oldest lie ever sold
All that glitters must be gold

Your velvet voice is a thing to hear
Warm tones punctuated by a hearty laugh
Not too alto, not too soprano
A pleasant flourish atop the verse

The saddest story ever told
All who lie must be bold

If everyone who knew you even a bit
Knew what lies behind
Smiles so wide and pleasant songs
They'd question their very ears

London fog

Somewhere in time the castle's carousel spins
Counter-clockwise revolutions reveal our Rochester

Colors bend, melt at the edges like mold on aging photos
Shapes fade into each other, focus-free and unforced

Dreaming back on days abroad it's wistful to see it
Through the prism of the girl in the London fog

Homework dates and post-test 'how did you do'
Easy laughs over pints at the pub (was it Chard for you?)

Theatre seats far up in the heavens did we ascend
And in December, a fateful stroll in Queen's Row

No, the glasses aren't rosy, the eyes bloodshot red
Straining to burn in the happy times I know we spent

Hapless in this hall of moments, I'd love to loiter
But long shadows haze over the real you, sans me

A closer reflection reveals the stories you told
Of love lost and parental disapproval displayed

When all you wanted was your first love
To have, to hold, and quite possibly, to wed

Just as I wanted with you, but, of course, too young
To fathom first love may not be found in a Fuller's pub

Too naive to know when all is done and said
I hope you've found true happiness in my stead

The castle walls stand strong in fading memory's light
The carousel cries out an ever familiar chant

That is your laugh, uncontained by your smiling lips,
Filling the misty night with the spirit of you

Whether in place or time, in dreams or memories
We'll always meet in the midst of the London fog

.: London, England :.

Inscription from a real book
regrettably not purchased

Mabel
Xmas 1912.
Snence it vanishes
get this
K. (illegible)

LONDON
VANISHED & VANISHING

Attention

You look down at your phone and throw your eyebrows
I don't know what you're saying on the inside
but out loud you say...
I don't get why he doesn't take the hint

I would've loved to have known more about that hint—
Was it smooth, bumpy, spiky or prickly
Did it smell like lilacs in spring or belching beaver farts
Was it the size of an 18-wheeler barreling over a bridge
Or a fuzzy little pika in the highest alpine forest
Was it loud and proud like a peacock
Or stealthy like the slithering of a serpent
Would it announce its presence like a royal court herald
Or tap lightly on the collar and whisper gently in your ear

I wish I'd understood more about that hint
Because when it was floated out in front of me
I missed it like the spectre it was, all silent signals
Lost upon layers of me just 'not getting it'

Hindsight is a beautiful thing, so when I looked back
I did feel something invisible in the air
After all those unreturned calls and texts
I realized that was the ghost you placed there

That thing I asked you not to do

I
The silverware shines, the stemware rings
A waitress rests her palm on my shoulder
Seated, stateless, I barely notice
I'm staring, hungry yet sated, across the table

A moment passes by, a pregnant moment
Which births a small revelation
Followed by a smaller request
One which, I hope, had hit its mark

Still smiling, your eyes seem to answer yes
Restaurant murmurs overshadow our talk
My mumbles gets lost in a montage
But then again, blushes are audible too

This scene is a beautiful regret

II

It takes mere months to discover I'm mistaken
Confusing nervous smiles for understanding
I've discovered is not just for rookies
And I begin to wonder about my small request

Messages left to calls returned, the ratio feels wrong
Kind remembrances have aged unkindly
I have fallen prey to the oldest foible
Foolishness festers at the feet of your silence

Two years later, countless lunches seem an aeon
Through the silence I recall the hand on my shoulder
And wonder whether it was a warning,
A pleasantry or an empathic understanding.

Was I wrong to think so highly of you?

Amor

hand on my throat, i'm in heaven
boot grinding my chest, i'm breathless

who cares about the marks it leaves
your size 8 1/2 imprints in red

horrified, your family pulls me out
what do i care, there's not much to surmount

you're good with words, orders even more
borders break easily with just the right gun

how long did it finally take? you're surprised they ask
when i didn't need rouge for Saturday mass

pardon my tone, blessed Father, sarcasm is sacred
it hurts more to repent, as a young fool i was taken

in the heat and dust, i succumbed to lust
and the offer of a life to live with my son in trust

but love in a tornado is sad to behold
from the outside just screams and fists uncontrolled

i ache now to realize the life i proclaimed
was just child abuse by another name

Boomerang

Last week you were in love with me
This week it's too much

Before midnight you were hating him
After the stroke your retraction hurts

Yesterday you trusted your instincts
Today they are suspect?

In the old year we consciously coupled
In the new we are caring strangers

Time has never seemed painful
Then again, neither did you

.: Santa Ana, CA :.

God gives you one face...

The deep

Shattered mirror fragments sear,
Clenched shards bleed a river of fear
Tattered hands fumble and grasp,
Clutching at frightened reflections
Of wrath, of wrong, of wanting.

Shuddering, we wreath a passionless
Tango á deux, a coupling turned cold
Our mission long absent from view,
Our parting long overdue.

We climb the deep, dearest,
In search of crags, crevices,
Bleeding hands, grasping blindly
Groping around the edges of a grave
Finding only roots of despair.

We climb the deep, dearest, as surely
As paired together we weep in secret
Silence, deafness, stillness.
Yes, love, we climb.

The coming war

From Adam's rib to Achilles heel
Your saga has been writ
In blood and yet still

First salvo was the salve
Brooch shaped or no
The choker clutches by half

What should be held dear
Not adorned or draped
Round a waifs waist

God damns the fear that swells
In your blessed throat
The words tell a bloody tale

Dropped to the floor when rapt
Upon man's menace or malice
Your innate strength sapped or slapped

Meek is the part men wish you to play
Tipping the scale to a minor pitch
Notes dipped in rancor harmonically

Matters not if you're Gen X Y or Z
You're all an unfortunate part
Of the same age-old cursed melody

Man's myth, ribs, heels in rhyme and art
Bloated, he boasts a hymn to him
And you, secondary citizen of earth,

Must assuage first or perhaps auger
A detente, a chill, or a Pax Romana
Whatever raging fists cannot render

The coming war, whether in silence or screams
Starts with words womb deep
'I fear not blood nor do I pander peace'

Gemini suns

Madame, *pardonne moi*, mademoiselle,
We are far too alike, I can tell

Est votre plage très jolie?
Another secret between you and me

Tu te chantes une douce chanson
A solemn hymn to him, trite only to some

La fraternité c'est bien pour l'idéaliste
My dear, your trust would pierce the lids of any pessimist

Tu t'enfuis quand le défi commence
"But I'm in love," *toujours* the weakest defense

The girl with the yellow scarf

Tap, tap, tap says acrylic on lacquered wood
Precious doe caught in the headlights
You stare disinterestedly ahead
Counter-culture inamorata

You scan the reading room for a pulse and find it—
Les artistes unabashéd in black,
The eccentric actress with props and fears in tow
The name dropper selling hints of immortality
The confectioner, the pro, the long-winded,
None so much as tempt your wide eyes

Opting for more, you push aside
Your yellow scarf and choose a random mark
As if floating, you glide towards a hapless man
A still life save the apple in his quivering left hand
Salomé-like, your dance is a warning
Extending a ruby-bejeweled finger, caressing his
Pressed suit, you move closer, bending lips to ear,
Mantra-like, you coolly intone—
"Andre Breton, Andre Breton."

.: San Marino, CA :.

Diana or Eurydice?

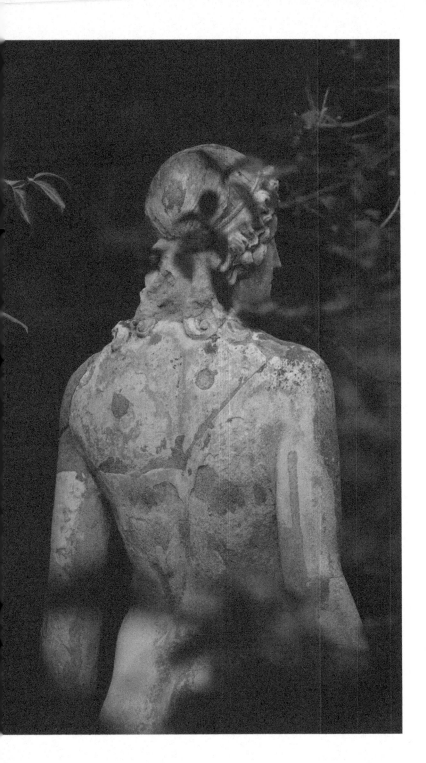

Warrior

brow furrowed o'er beautiful bullets betray any signs of cynic
a victors voice, at times calm, others clarion, always an aria
a physique mightily flexed, a force one should never beset
bringer of war, beware the sage and savage Athena
protector of the weak, pivoting cat-like when she must kill
her arms a bridge, girded, outstretched like giant colossi
strength enough for all, the proud, the needy, all are kin
blessed am i to know a warrior such as she, mighty Minerva

Helpless

How can i write about something I'll never know
To be filled with a miracle that grows

In silence and mirth blossoms a miraculous birth
Feted for years, a sacred shrine

Yet in tears and muffled screams
Others are filled with a void so supreme

It drowns out voices, outside and in
Leaves no waking peace, just fear of sin

Every life creates a mother no matter the term
Their decisions twist and turn on the wing of a tern

I glimpse its flight from afar as it recedes
How wingless the tacet spectator I must be

28: a declaration

I am a force to be reckoned with
My body outgrown my childish years
Rough edges become curves, a delight to men
But they do not see me

I am more than ten digits
More than tits and a handful of ass
More than idle barroom banter
You would hope define me

I am a phoenix among the cocks and hens
Talk to me a minute and you'll see—
As long as conversation isn't a contrivance
And intimidation isn't your cup of tea

An unoffered piece of flesh in your hands
Is your version of risk, I know how you think—
Try tickling my intellect, not any part
Of what you think constitutes my fancy

I have diaries full of hopes and childhood dreams
And day-by-fucking-day I make the ink come alive
What's sporting for me is how clever you can be
And if you take your time you may get the key

I am Eros and Ego and Medusa (just test my wrath)
Caring and calmness and civility to more than some
Worthy of honor and respect and deservedly so
Having been loved, I can love—I know where to go

.: Long Beach, CA :.

Den of thieves

Et tu Brute?

a group of friends, some fake some not
more than a few have already tied the knot

parties and fetes and wine nights galore
conversation crackled, no sign of a snore

we thought it'd never end, the times were so good
some hardly noticed a quiet creeping mood

those who did heard the sound of triangles tinkling
luckily so many didn't really have an inkling

some deep inside the party assured they could be trusted
but in time tea was spilled and secrets were busted

everyone looked for culprits, ceaseless was the hunt
in the end naught was revealed, perhaps it was a stunt?

or is it that everyone befriends Judas at least once in their life
masquerading as an acquaintance, friend or a wife

Instapoetry

What do you call a friend
who accepts information about you
half (or most) of which is untrue,
spilled like tea without any responsibility
to you or (God knows) how many pair of ears

What do you call a friend
who doesn't tell you what they've heard
they just inch away, extra beats between texts
thumbs and icons replace full sentences
(the ghosting isn't far behind)

What do you call a friend
who doesn't defend you
who doesn't question the source
who doesn't even bother to check the facts

What do you call...fuck—
You don't call them a friend.

28: a revocation

A fire within, reason without
Head first you plunge without reasonable doubt
A hero to me at first you seemed
How wrong was i when at last i can see

Behind the smile a silhouette
Shadows of your other self
Moving in rhymes as men's heads sway
Laughing glances from others do betray

Everyone has virtue that's easy to say
Harder to prove it as you lie away
The same mouth breeds half truths
I guess its not as shocking as it sounds

Eager fool i am, it was folly to confuse
The right mixture of pop culture psyche
Late night cabernet and a wise pose
With empathy as sina que non

Are you laughing still as the child would?
Or have you moved on, headfast and steadfast?
Proffering slivers of kindness and calling it love
Quixote, my dear, it's not just me

You know best of all the pain of being an object
Yet as best you tried, the empath becomes the builder
Of webs and clubs and secret societies
Far more childish than your twenty-eight years ought to be

You deserve better

Ear to ear smiles and velvet thighs
Everyday thongs and creative sing-alongs
Moroccan brown-eyed hues...
Baby, he doesn't deserve you

Damask in jade, you stroll the colonnade
Soaking in the sun, your fun has just begun
But when the dark clouds come into view...
Dearest one, what's he doing to you?

Your strong caress helps relieve his stress
Nimble fingers make the pleasure linger
When the tides turn and you want to screw...
Sweetie, what will he do for you?

Lonely kingdom

you make the rules
i can never argue
you never budge in your position
i can try logic
you swat away with exceptions
i can say this is the way you are
you say i'll never know
i say how typical a sign
you say this is the way i am
i say love is more than acceptance
you say i don't make the rules
i say that's not what this all about
you say you can't talk about this anymore
i say it's too late at night to wage war
you say there's nothing to discuss
i say what a barren landscape you rule over

.: Somewhere in CA :.

The road to rebirth

The silence

Silence used as a shield defends
It all depends on your ability to pretend

Questions like arrows whiz quickly by
Turning the other cheek seems just fine

When pressed to explain why you feel rushed
Your cherubic cheeks churns a genial flush

Words can be wrong so 'tis better to feign
A basic understanding of the human game

Silence as a drawn sword can also defend
Against feelings you say you can't seem to stand

Tacet

Hands half-a-foot across the table
Over faraway restaurant murmurs
Our mouths motionless—
I hear you loud and clear

Locked in silence, I search your eyes
Deep mahogany distracts from a quiver
(Did you know your right eye is darker than your left?)
And a smile would reveal a river of emotions

A moment and a space, you said
A chasm in time, it feels
I tried not to stare, but it's too late
I fell into your eye's cosmos

311

If I had known that morning you would have come
I would have held my breath and stayed
Eager for something magical to happen

If I had known you would have looked at me the way you do
I could have braced for a force of nature
I was not prepared for

Your stare is lethal in its depth and intensity
Our quiet, breathless moments reveal a storm
Hush now, the words we don't need to speak…

Poetry does not serve in the heat of our moment
Two worlds, one dying, the other doomed
Bridged by passion, guilt at every guidepost

If I had known your rage I would have held you tighter
Could have soothed every morning's dull ache
If only you would have let me

If I would have known I would fall so hard
I would have slid off the lock, opened the door
And jumped into your heart just once more

Awakened

Ask me now if I had known
And I would have said no—
Perhaps after the moment's trance,
After the clicking clock slows to a crawl,
Kindred one, I am trapped in the gravity of your glance
And my hearts ashram rendered to dust.

Since you were unforeseen, your smiles hid secrets—
Visions of the past, promises of the future
All sun-drenched, starlit, soul-filled
As though written in the most beautiful code
Garlands writhe between strands of your hair
As if leg-locked in Grecian repose.
Troilus to your Cressida, I court your love.

Heaven scent, spiced vanilla, coconut flakes
And coriander, clasps of cinnamon and cumin—
I breathe you in—unstoppable aroma, sated by nothing.

Ask me now if I had seen
And I would have said no—
Save the smile, the glowing eyes, the knowing.
How scared and scarred my heart has been to miss
Chance encounters with you.
Hold fast love—through granite falls rivulets of hope
As a hardened heart awakens from an aeon sleep,
Ready to climb, eager to fight,
Yearning to fly.

You

Ear to ear sunshine
Glowing eyes to match
Set fire to the room with a glance

Slivered scents of vanilla
Surround your knowing gaze
As safely I settle into your stare

Long, luxurious ravens' hair
Flows over shoulder and breast
Heave a sigh for me, breathe me in

Delicately parted lips reveal much
A glint of a grin lies just beyond
I follow it to your eyes' smile

Color cascades from your neck
Splashes of sage, copper and crème
Bejeweled in fuchsia and crimson

A coronation of grace and beauty
Filled by God's details, rightly chosen
Divine yet mortal, the muse that is you

.: Long Beach, CA :.

A new chapter

Year of the lotus

Mud-born, sun-kissed blossom
Asks the night to renew
In water the warm days'
Noise and sweat.

That beauty is birthed in murk
Under a canopy of darkness
Mystifies reason
Signals rebirth
Even as it dies daily.

Purity in chaos—
Yes, veritably, love,
An apt descriptor,
Requiem in bello.

Kindred, caring, blind souls
Afloat on a pond of dreams
Rainwater dabbing at the blossom pads
That buoy us above the unseen depths—
Hold fast, love, renewal comes
At night, the evening dew our sacrament.

How transfiguring, the year of the lotus—
On a basin of fantasy I fan out and float,
Offering up myself to your sun, closing my eyes as
Nighttime becomes a nocturne, chanting your name.

Parting

Choked back in the throat
sugar cubes with course edges
scraping, scraping, never dulling

stitched lips, blood congeals
as mumbles clot, cannot recite
vinegar coated lies

lids seared, then *chien*-like split
cannot recant the seen,
even though the seer is blind

needle pricks in every orifice
parting meant not offering happiness
only courage not to return to this moment

Momentos

Teasingly tangible, lacy and sheer
Must I be careful and keep it near?

Thousands of words, my my picture this
Expressions more fleeting than a kiss

Moving images oh dear how they move me
Almost as though i'll ne'er be rid of thee

Treasures once lost should surely be found
Just like those I gave you, lest theories abound

Narcissus

I know you don't think he's capable of harming
Because, hey ladies, narcissists are charming

San Simeon

Listen to the music of the waves at night
It obliterates every other sound
A melody felt beneath the belly of the ground

The closer you get, the louder I have to yell
It envelopes all, so much more when you're not around
A force my burden to be laid at the edge of sand

Surf roars at me, sans you
A hearts cry twice as cruel
Stupid and blythe am I le fou

Thank God you can't hear me
Amidst the roar my anguish
Pity only a part of me wishes you can't

My words are lightning
The tide thunders back
I despise its response

Surf breaks hard upon a rock
Bigger than the Morro
You've lead me here before

It's not higher than I, it's further
Legless in the strand, I struggle to sync
Cursing the roar, the tide, all traces of you
You've lead me here before

.: San Simeon, CA :.

Healing

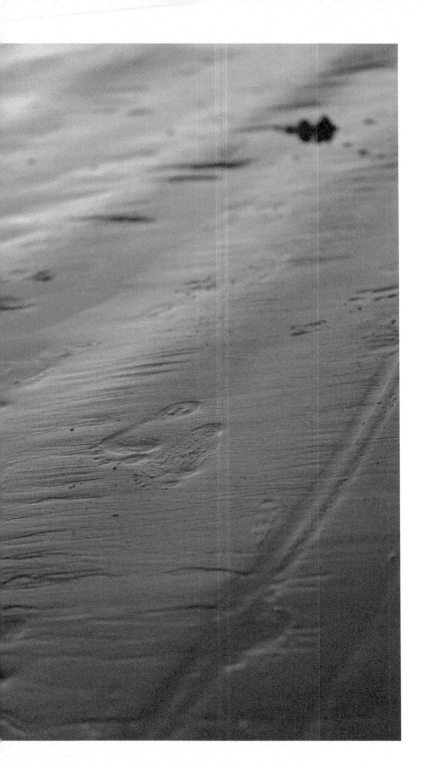

Page 84

Everything's worse when you're back with him
(yes, of course, I would say worse)
The inquisition is not Spanish, it's universal
The suspicion, the mistrust, the unspoken

Of course it's worse
You're not with me
You went back to prove something to yourself
And be punished in the process

I pray to my God, you pray to yours
(he wishes that was him)
Which one will bring you to me faster?
And are you even praying?

I cringe thinking that
I'm not supposed to lose my faith
Only my patience
Waiting for you

A love like ours (by rights) isn't supposed to exist
Our connection is cosmos
Want me to prove it?
Come close and let me hug your waste

I love watching you melt
As you exhale into me
Do you have that with him?
I know the answer

Olde English

It quite the conundrum, isn't it?
The fact you married a *cunt*

You must have forgotten that all-important part
Whilst writing your wedding vows

Was it her stupidity that blinded you?
Those qualities are married in your mind, nés pa?

Stupid cunt was it?
No no, 'twas something else…

Do you take her, this *stupid cunt*, to have and to hold,
In sickness and in health, til disappointment do you part?

Your disappointment, of course—how could anyone intelligent
Not see they must navigate your moods, your manners

Read your mind, be silent at just the right time, be keenly
Aware of the volcano within, ready to erupt at any moment

Ah, I remember now—*stupid fucking cunt*—that was it!
Such a melodious ring to it when spoken with such commitment

Why would you leave those precious words out of your wedding vows
When you give yourself permission to use them on any given day?

Just as the tallest most regal trees need water for roots,
Your speedy growth was watered with her tears

The seeds were planted long ago, and my how you tower
Above us all, arms outstretched, a canopy shielding you from truth

Sadly the metaphor is lost—looking down on us all
Means you know many more *stupid fucking cunts* in your life

Of course, it wouldn't occur you'd said anything wrong,
You are the chosen steward of ancient, sacred words

The power you alone are blessed to use and command
Judgement is mine, thus sayeth the man

Who tolerates his wife, who corrects her all her life
Who shows her he's the one, especially in front of their son

You can't fuck your way out of everything

the job you're always looking for but never find
the food that's prepped for only you
the mileage saved as the perpetual passenger
the smiles for others as they pass through

the lingering glances at the other end
the dryness in my mouth after unanswered calls
the silence at dinner dates so many years along
the token smile when i sense you fall

the life that's lived alone because of your "busy"
the shadow in your smile fueled by need
the lies you tell others to make yourself better
the lies i believe because they end in '...but i love you'

Eurydice

Jokes at your expense
Private jokes in public view
Rugs ripped out from underneath
After all, it's his child too

Kinder words he saves for other belles
Whether you're in view or no
And any offense easily smoothed
He knows you're afraid to go

Barbed words bring forth blood
A mortal wound in the marital keep
It could be triaged, but it's twisted steel
You breath your last and yet you don't leave

A demi demise doesn't send you to the dark
You realize you've married Orpheus—
Except he wouldn't go into hell for you,
Why do you give him heaven?

.: Long Beach, CA :.

Three colors, all blue

Cowards & queens

Annointed in love and so quickly to bed
You know him so little yet you garland his head
'Tis pity in coronation he never grasps the jest
Nor any of your needs when first you met

A queen lays astride in the court of *l'amour fou*
No need for an almoner, there's a knight in view
He quickly sees the king as the royal jest
Yet you sire *le roi's* progeny in his stead

Courtesan or coward, count on *le conte*
To press whate'er flesh is closest, ne'er best
L'ombre d'un roi remands you of all joy
Issues edicts, commands you to act like his toy

Flirts and smiles to the side, he'll never surmise
The depth of deception you'll never decry
As your knight departs, ne'er reveal the mark
Le roi long ago left, as you *baise le patriarche*

Day x without me

Day 1
Cut loose, the current crashes against the dinghy
The severed line cracking whip-like over the waves

Standing is simple, says i, as i and i stumble
Sick from spinning, i wretch into dark water

Day 13
E'en from afar the knife reflects the moonlight
Soaking, soggy, i clench at frayed ends

These remnants are my rancor
Reaching out into the abyss

Day 39
You dismissed the lifeboat
Before you even measured the jump
You said you dropped the knife in the deep
After the cut...in nightmares i see it

Day 62
It feels as if i've spent an age regaining balance
But it's only been two damn months

Day 77
You at the bow, me at the stern, both in turn
Buoying amidst the ballast beaming in the sun

Daydreams, like delusions, are a dreadful lie
Clutching still to the vest lest one of us cry

Day 142
The fog of war has faded, detente sadly begun
From the bow your gaze wasn't on me, 'twas beyond

I'm sorry now not to tell the wounds were so dire
But even pretty criers stream tears of fire

Day 211
Looking back, what brought you there?
Gazing adoration, reading the tiny curl of your lip

Would it have gotten old?

Clever is your smile, whether a grin or a disguise
You row back to a marriage built on abuse and lies

How is life without me...fool that i love[d]?

D is for delusion

A is for the abuse i daily choose to take
B is for the breakup i sorely wish to make

C is for the choice word my husband calls me
D is for the delusion my friends want me to see

E is the nagging empty i feel at home
F is the fear i'll never be left alone

G belongs to the gal that finally made me cry
H is for the hugs she gave to make me feel alive

I is for this invalid who wants to learn to walk
J is the jokes she makes as we laugh and talk

King is for the king that should be deposed
L is the lioness inside that craves to be bold

M is for the marriage i'm too afraid to leave
N is for the nervousness that always nags at me

O is for the olive branch that never was received
P is for perfection which i never seem to achieve

Q is for the quagmire of my deepest hopes and dreams
R is for redemption which always seems to recede

S is for the sex you want as it unsexes me
T is the tree of life that blossoms underneath

U is for the unborn for which i carry seed
V is for the victims in this melodic tryst

W is a witness when i finally discover peace
X however marks the spots where you berated me

Y is the you i must learn to live without
Z is the zephyr wind your cruelty brings about

Ozymandias

Living statue, exposed at the neck above shifting sands
Pristine and polished after a passing maelstrom

The sun obscures the tiny cracks across the face
Zigzagging from head to unseen foot

If viewed up close, the fractures would seem rivers
And if touched, they'd surely crack and crumble

Viewed from afar the rivers merge into a petit pattern
Alluring yet hard to discern through squinting eyes

Who knows how far down the damage goes
A puzzle box buried under time

Viewed with wounded eyes who can tell if
This colussus is being interred or exhumed

Cariño

Roackaby baby don't you dare lie
Mama's off the ropes, gonna cut you right
Mama's raging, don't you run from the fight
Your head's in my hands, wish you could die?

Cariño don't move, you coward piece of shit
Your puta left, she didn't catch your drift
My rage is fire, ashes your gift
Watch me cheat on you, our cradle can split.

.: Long Beach, CA :.

More than it seems

Blank spaces

I know you still love me
  know you still love
I   you still
I know you
I know
I
I ache
I ache now
I ache now more
I ache   more than
I ache now more than ever

Love will guide us home
Love will guide us
Love will guide
        will
Love
Love will
Love will tear
Love will tear us
Love   tear us to
Love will   us to pieces

You said you'd always love me
        said you'd always love
You said you'd always
You said you'd
You said
You
You are
You are a
You are a part
You are   of
You are a part of me

Please don't say there's   fish
Please don't say there's more
Please don't say there's
Please don't say
Please don't
Please
Stay
Stay stronger
Stay stronger than
Stay stronger   me
Stay stronger than   please

Angkor Wat

Soul prone, head floating,
Feet planted yet shaking in the dirt
Leaning forward, I cup my hands
And groan a prayer—dear God
Please shoulder my secret

Furrowing forehead
Into granite, I try not to
Cry grist into my eyes

I fail

Whispers are bullets
Quietly sprayed
Over the pain of time
I have no aim for mine

A clump of dirt packs it all in
The crafted lies, the naked truth
The hidden joys, the open wounds
All proof of a love it aches to inter

About the Author

Paul J. Bean was born and raised in Grand Rapids, Michigan. After high school, Paul attended Western Michigan University where he studied English Literature and Theatre. While in college, he wrote and produced two one-act plays and a short film, *Thirteen*. After graduating, Paul moved to California and continued to write while working as a creative executive in marketing and advertising.

In 2008, Paul published his first book of poetry, *Confessions of a Latter-Day Cynic*, which was well received. He is currently working on several literary projects, including a new screenplay, a play about modern politics and an episodic streaming series based on his years in corporate America.

In his spare time, Paul enjoys movies and film studies, live jazz, travelling to foreign shores, photography and architecture.

Author's Note

Several of the poems in the book deal with some difficult issues, including domestic violence and child abuse.

National Domestic Violence Hotline
Hours: 24/7
Languages: English, Spanish and 200+ *(through interpretation service)*

Call: 800-799-7233
SMS: Text START to 88788

Ten percent of book profits will be donated to the
Anne Douglas Center for Women at the Los Angeles Mission

More information: https://losangelesmission.org

Ten percent of book profits will be donated to
Su Casa — Ending Domestic Violence

More information: https://sucasadv.org

Made in the USA
Las Vegas, NV
17 January 2024

84516676R00069